CW00370202

GREAT BRITISH
Baking
Cakes & Breads

Annie Low

GREAT BRITISH
Baking
Cakes & Breads

First published in the UK in 2014

© Demand Media Limited 2014

www.demand-media.co.uk

Printed and bound in Europe

ISBN 978-1-910270-20-2

Contents

Chapter 1

Introduction

Ever since I was a child baking with my mother, I was fascinated by the magic of baking. How is it that the three main ingredients of almost all things baked, sugar, butter and flour, can you make so many different things - cakes, scones, biscuits, pastry, & breads? The list is almost endless and it is only subtle variations in the quantities used, the way they are prepared and then mixed with other ingredients, that makes a world of difference in the finished product. Be it a light fluffy sponge cake or a dense chocolate torte, it is only the baker's artistry that makes the difference.

Many people are baffled by baking for just this reason and can be reluctant to bake for fear of getting it wrong. However whatever the science behind it may be, with clear instructions and a little attention to detail anyone can bake delicious things. This little book of Great British Baking is both a starting point for novice bakers as well as an inspiration for more experienced cooks to get back into their pinnie and, maybe, try something different.

In selecting the twenty recipes for this book, I have tried to include something that will appeal to everyone as well as representing a broad spectrum of sweet and savoury items. Each recipe is clearly laid out and explained step by step to make what we hope will be a foolproof guide.

Happy baking!

Now it's my children who are fascinated by the magic of baking!

BASIC WHITE BREAD

Ingredients...

Makes a 2lb loaf

1 egg
1 egg yolk
200ml (7 fl oz) lukewarm water
500g (1lb 2oz) strong white flour
1 tsp salt

2 tsp sugar
1 tsp easy-blend dried yeast
25g (1oz) butter
Sunflower oil (for greasing)

Preparation...

Pre-heat your oven to 220°C (425°F) Gas Mark 7,
and lightly grease a 900g (2lb) loaf tin.

TIP: To make sure the bread is cooked, carefully turn the loaf out of the tin, tap the base with your knuckles – it should sound hollow.

Equipment needed...

7 ITEMS

Large Mixing Bowl
Medium Mixing Bowl
Small Mixing Bowl
Pastry Brush
Tea Towel
2 lb Loaf Tin
Cooling Rack

Method...

1

Place the egg and egg yolk in a bowl and beat lightly, and add enough lukewarm water to make it up to 300ml (10 fl oz), and stir.

2

Put the flour, salt, sugar and yeast into a large bowl, add the butter.

3

Rub the butter in with your fingertips until the mixture resembles breadcrumbs.

4

Make a well in the centre and add the egg liquid and mix until to a smooth dough.

BASIC WHITE BREAD

5

Lightly flour your work surface and turn out the dough, and knead well for about 5-10 minutes until smooth.

6

Shape the dough into a ball and place into a mixing bowl greased with oil.

7

Cover the bowl with a damp cloth and leave to rise in a warm place for about 1 hour, until the dough has doubled in size.

8

Knock down the dough, then turn out onto a lightly floured work surface and knead for 1 minute.

9

Shape the dough to the same size as the tin, place it inside, cover and leave to rise for about 30 minutes until double in size.

10

Put the tin in the preheated oven and bake for 30 minutes until golden. Turn out onto a wire rack to cool.

Then enjoy!

PLAITED POPPY SEED LOAF

Ingredients...

225g (8oz) strong White Flour
1 tsp salt
2 tbsp skimmed milk powder
1 tbsp caster sugar
1 tsp dried yeast

175ml (6 fl oz) lukewarm water
2 tbsp vegetable oil
5 tbsp poppy seeds

Glaze: 1 tbsp milk
2 tbsp poppy seeds

Preparation...

Pre-heat your oven to 200°C (400°F), Gas Mark 6,
and brush a baking tray with oil.

Equipment needed...

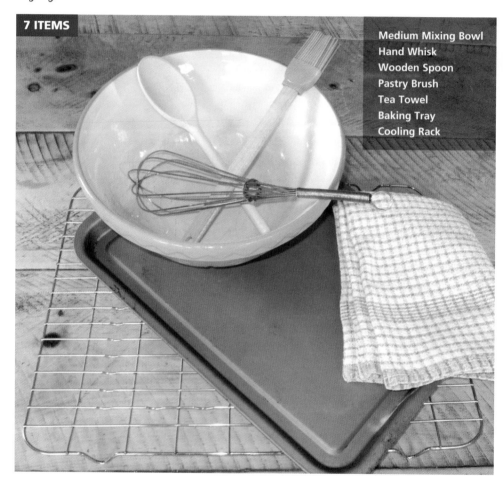

7 ITEMS

Medium Mixing Bowl
Hand Whisk
Wooden Spoon
Pastry Brush
Tea Towel
Baking Tray
Cooling Rack

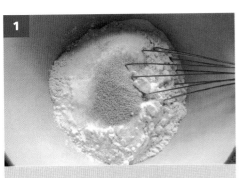

In a large mixing bowl, sift the flour and add the salt, skimmed milk powder, castor sugar and yeast.

Make a well in the centre of the flour and add the water and oil.

Mix together with a spoon until the dough comes together, then add the poppy seeds. Tip the dough onto a floured work surface and kneed with your hands for about 5-10 minutes until smooth and elastic.

PLAITED POPPY SEED LOAF

4 Brush the bowl with oil and put the dough inside.

5 Cover with a damp towel and leave to rise in a warm place for 1 hour, until double in size.

6 Knock down and turn the dough out onto a floured work surface, and knead for about 1 minute.

Divide the dough into three equal pieces and shape to about 10-12 inches long.

Plait the dough and place onto the prepared baking tray, cover with a damp cloth and leave to rise in a warm place for 30 minutes or until double in size.

Brush the plait with the milk and sprinkle lightly with poppy seeds, and bake in the pre-heated oven for 30-35 minutes until golden.

Now slice, butter & enjoy!

FOCCACIA BREAD

Ingredients...

Makes 1 loaf

450g (1lb) strong white flour
7g sachet of dried yeast
1 tsp salt
2 tbsp olive oil
300ml (10 fl oz) lukewarm water

Topping:
1 tbsp olive oil
2 garlic cloves, crushed
2 stalks of fresh rosemary,
leaves removed
1 tsp sea salt for scattering

Preparation...

Pre-heat the oven to 200°C (400°F), Gas Mark 6.

TIP: This recipe is best served whilst still warm.

Equipment needed...

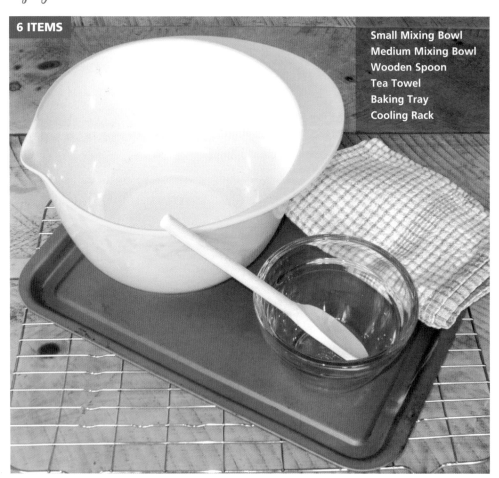

6 ITEMS

Small Mixing Bowl
Medium Mixing Bowl
Wooden Spoon
Tea Towel
Baking Tray
Cooling Rack

Method...

FOCCACIA BREAD

1

In a small bowl prepare the topping, by mixing together the olive oil, garlic and rosemary and set aside.

2

Put the flour, yeast and salt into a medium sized bowl and mix together, then add the oil and water and mix to a soft dough.

3

Turn out onto a lightly floured work surface and knead gently for about 10 minutes until smooth.

FOCCACIA BREAD

4

Put the dough into a large bowl, lightly greased with oil, cover with a damp cloth and leave in a warm place for about 1 hour until double in size.

5

Carefully tip the dough onto a lightly floured work surface and knead for a couple of times, being careful not to knock out the air too much.

6

Place the dough onto large greased baking tray and gently roll and gently pull dough to a rectangle about 30 x 23cm (12 x 9 inches).

7

With your finger make dimples into the dough.

8

Brush the dough with the topping mixture, and pop it into the pre-heated oven for 20-25 minutes until golden. Drizzle with any remaining oil and transfer to a wire rack to cool.

Enjoy while warm!

CINNAMON ROLLS

Ingredients...

350g (12oz) self raising flour
2 tbsp caster sugar
1/4 tsp salt
1 tsp ground cinnamon
100g (3¹/₂ oz) butter, melted
2 egg yolks
200ml (6¹/₂ fl oz) milk

Filling:
1 tsp ground cinnamon
55g (2oz) soft light brown sugar
2 tbsp caster sugar
1 tbsp butter, melted

Icing:
125g (4¹/₂ oz) icing sugar, sifted
2-3 tsp hot water

Preparation...

Pre-heat the oven to 180°C (350°F), Gas Mark 4, and grease a 23cm (9 inch) round cake tin and place a disc of parchment paper in the bottom.

TIP: This recipe is best served whilst still warm.

Equipment needed...

Wooden Spoon
Small Mixing Bowls x 2
Hand Whisk x 2
Medium Mixing Bowls x 2
Rolling Pin
Baking Parchment/
Greaseproof Paper
Pastry Brush
23cm (9 inch) round cake tin
Cooling Rack

1

For the filling, mix together the melted butter, sugars and cinnamon in a small bowl and set aside.

2

In a medium size mixing bowl, mix together the flour, caster sugar, salt and cinnamon.

3

In a smaller mixing bowl, whisk the melted butter, egg yolks and milk together until combined.

4

Make a well in the centre of the flour mix and add the buttery liquid and mix to form a soft dough.

CINNAMON ROLLS

5

Turn the dough out onto a lightly floured work surface and knead gently. Place the dough onto a large sheet of baking parchment and sprinkle with flour. Roll the dough out to approximately 30 x 25 cm (12 x 10 inches).

6

Sprinkle the filling evenly over the dough and brush one end with milk.

7

Lift the paper's edge furthest away from you and pull towards you rolling up the dough in the process, sealing at the dampened edge.

8

Cut the log into eight even size pieces with a sharp knife and place into the prepared tin. Brush the tops of the rolls with a little milk and pop the tin into the oven for 30-35 minutes, or until lightly brown.

Remove from the oven and leave to cool in the tin for 5 minutes before transferring to a wire rack.

Sift the icing sugar into a bowl and add enough boiling water to make a thick paste. Mix well and then drizzle over the rolls.

Then enjoy!

CHEESE TWISTS

Ingredients...

1 pkt of ready made puff pastry
200g (7oz) strong cheddar cheese
4 tbsp english mustard
2 tbsp milk
extra cheese for sprinkling

Preparation...

Pre-heat the oven to 200°C (400°F), Gas Mark 6.

TIP: These are perfect for snacks, picnics and school lunch boxes – my kids love them!

Equipment needed...

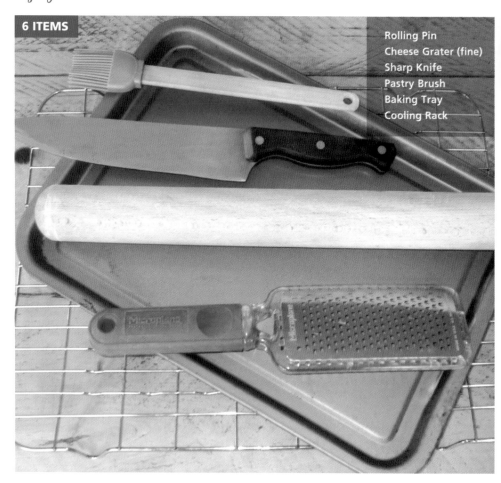

6 ITEMS

Rolling Pin
Cheese Grater (fine)
Sharp Knife
Pastry Brush
Baking Tray
Cooling Rack

Method...

1 Roll the pastry out to a square approximately 40 cm (16 inches) wide, and trim the edges.

2 Cut the pastry in half horizontally, and spread one of the halves with 2 tbsp of the mustard.

3 Finely grate half of the cheese and sprinkle over the pastry and gently press down onto the mustard.

CHEESE TWISTS

4

Cut the pastry into 2.5 cm (1 inch) strips.

5

Take two strips and baste one of them with milk. Put the other strip ontop and gently roll. Do this to the remaining strips.

6

Take two of the strips and pinch them together at the top. Twist together pinching the ends to secure.

Repeat this process with the remaining pastry. Baste them with a little milk and sprinkle with a little extra grated cheese.

7

Bake the twists in the pre-heated oven for 10-12 minutes until golden brown. Leave to cool on a wire rack.

Now its time to share!

VICTORIA SPONGE CAKE

Ingredients...

Makes a 20cm (8 inch) cake

225g (8oz) self raising flour
225g (8oz) caster sugar
225g (8oz) butter, softened
4 eggs
2 tsp baking powder

Filling:
5 tbsp raspberry or
strawberry jam
Icing sugar or caster sugar
to sprinke

Preparation...

Pre-heat the oven to 180°C (350°F), Gas Mark 4.

Equipment needed...

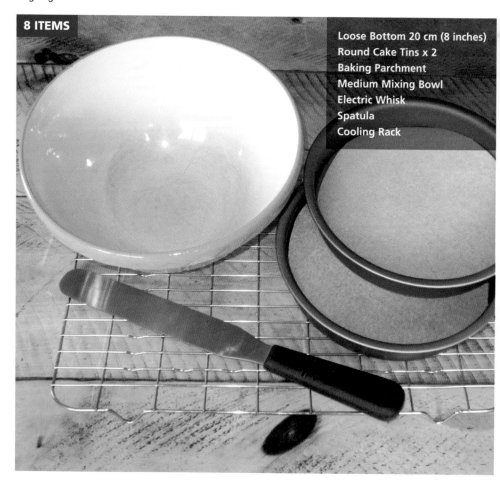

8 ITEMS

Loose Bottom 20 cm (8 inches)
Round Cake Tins x 2
Baking Parchment
Medium Mixing Bowl
Electric Whisk
Spatula
Cooling Rack

Method...

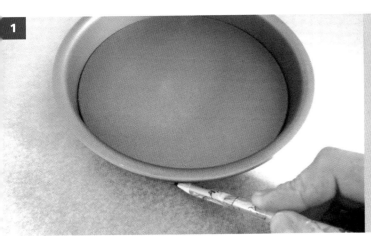

1

Grease two 20cm (9 inch) sandwich tins and line the bases with parchment paper.

2

Whisk the butter in a medium sized mixing bowl until smooth.

3

Add the sugar and whisk until light and creamy.

VICTORIA SPONGE CAKE

4

Add one egg at a time and whisk until well combined.

5

Gently whisk in the flour and baking powder.

6

Divide the mixture between the two tins and bake in the pre-heated oven for 20-25 mins until golden or until a skewer comes clean once inserted.

7

Leave the cakes to cool in the tin for a few minutes and then turn out, peel off the parchment and leave to cool completely on a wire rack.

8

Sandwich the cakes together with jam and sprinkle with caster sugar or icing sugar depending on preference.

Then slice and enjoy!

STICKY GINGER CAKE

Ingredients...

Makes a 9 inch (23cm) square cake

300g (10½ oz) plain flour
1 tsp bicarbonate of soda
1 tsp ground cinnamon
3 tbsp ground ginger
65g (2oz) light soft brown sugar
105g (3½ oz) dark soft brown sugar
150g (5oz) butter
200g (7oz) golden syrup
200g (7oz) black treacle
2 eggs
250 ml (5 fl oz) milk

Preparation...

Pre-heat the oven to 170°C (350°F), Gas Mark 3, and line a 23cm (9 inch) square cake tin with parchment paper. Alternatively, you can use a silicone cake tin of the same size and do not need to line it.

TIP: This recipe is best made a couple of days before serving, to allow it to become really sticky! If you don't want to use Black Treacle you can you 350g of golden syrup instead but the cake won't be quite so sticky.

Equipment needed...

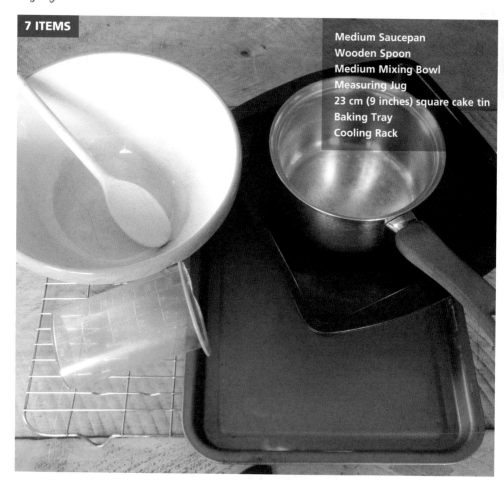

7 ITEMS

Medium Saucepan
Wooden Spoon
Medium Mixing Bowl
Measuring Jug
23 cm (9 inches) square cake tin
Baking Tray
Cooling Rack

1

Firstly, place the butter, golden syrup and black treacle into a saucepan and heat gently until the butter has melted.

2

In a large mixing bowl combine the flour, bicarbonate of soda, cinnamon, ginger and sugars, make a well in the centre and add the 2 eggs.

STICKY GINGER CAKE

With an electric whisk, mix the eggs into the floury mixture and slowly pour in the milk.

Then pour in the syrup liquid and whisk thoroughly.

5

Pour the liquid batter into the prepared tin and bake in the pre-heated oven for 40 minutes or until it has risen and is firm on to touch on the top.

6

Leave in the tin until cold. Once the cake is cold, take it out of the tin, wrap it tightly with cling film and leave in a cool place.

Wait a couple of days (if you can) to become really sticky!

INDULGENT CHOCOLATE CAKE

Ingredients...

Makes a 9 inch (23cm) cake

140g (5oz) plain chocolate
100ml (3½ fl oz) milk
2 tbsp cocoa powder
140g (5oz) butter
140g (5oz) soft dark brown sugar
3 eggs, separated
4 tbsp Greek Yoghurt
200g (7oz) plain flour
1 tsp bicarbonate of soda

Icing:
140g (5oz) plain chocolate
40g (1½ oz) cocoa powder
4 tbsp Greek yoghurt
1 tbsp golden syrup
40g (1½ oz) butter
4 tbsp water
200g (7oz) icing sugar

Preparation...

Pre-heat the oven to 160°C (325°F) Gas Mark 3, and grease two 23cm (9 inch) sandwich tins and line the bases with parchment paper.

Equipment needed...

9 ITEMS

Small Saucepan
Small (heatproof) Mixing Bowl
Medium Mixing Bowl
Electric Whisk
Silicone Scraper
9 inch (23 cm) loose bottom
Cake tins x 2
Baking Parchment
Wooden Spoon

Method...

1

Break the chocolate into small pieces and put them into a heatproof bowl with the milk and cocoa powder. Place the bowl over a saucepan of boiling water and stir until melted. Remove from the heat.

2

In a large mixing bowl beat the butter and sugar until pale and creamy.

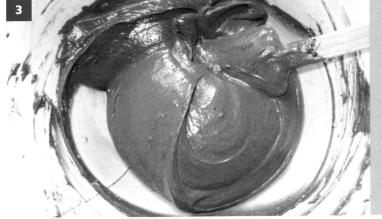

3

Add the egg yolks and greek yoghurt and mix well. Slowly add the melted chocolate stirring continuously.

INDULGENT CHOCOLATE CAKE

Sift the flour and bicarbonate of soda, and carefully fold into the mixture.

In a separate bowl whisk the egg whites until they form stiff peaks, and then fold them into the chocolate mixture.

Divide the mixture between the two tins, and bake in the preheated oven for about 20-30 minutes, or until risen and firm to touch. Cool in the tins before transferring to a wire rack.

7

For the icing, place the chocolate, cocoa powder, Greek yoghurt, golden syrup, butter and water into a saucepan and heat gently until melted.

8

Sift in the icing sugar and stir until smooth. Leave to cool, stirring occasionally, until the mixture begins to thicken and hold its shape.

9

Cut each cake in half horizontally to make four layers. Sandwich the cake with some of the icing and use the remaining icing to cover the tops and sides of the cake.

Now its time to indulge!

SCRUMPTIOUS CARROT CAKE

Ingredients...

Makes a 9 inch (23cm) round cake

275g (10oz) caster sugar
225ml (8 fl oz) sunflower oil
3 eggs
175g (6oz) self raising flour, sifted
1½ tsp baking powder
1½ tsp ground cinnamon
½ tsp ground gloves

½ tsp salt
225g (8oz) carrots, grated

Frosting:
150g (6oz) cream cheese
80g (3oz) unsalted butter
6 tbsp caster sugar

Preparation...

Pre-heat the oven to 175°C (350°F), Gas Mark 4, and grease and line a loose bottomed 20 cm (8 inch) deep cake tin with parchment paper.

Equipment needed...

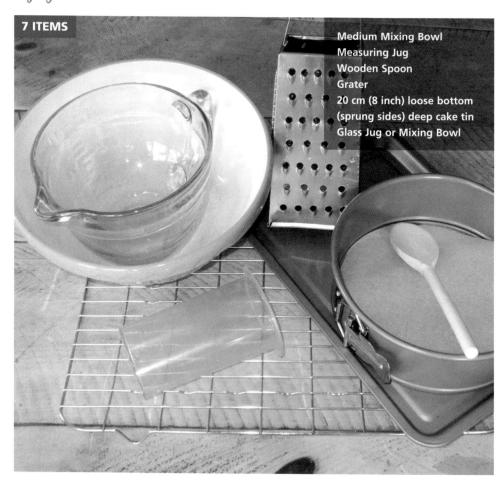

7 ITEMS

Medium Mixing Bowl
Measuring Jug
Wooden Spoon
Grater
20 cm (8 inch) loose bottom
(sprung sides) deep cake tin
Glass Jug or Mixing Bowl

Method...

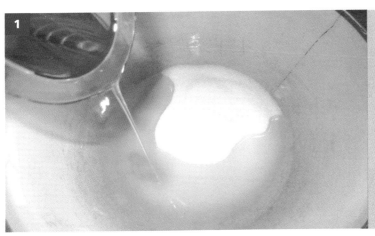

Place the sugar in a medium sized mixing bowl, stir in the oil and beat with a wooden spoon until well mixed.

Break one egg at a time into the sugary oil mixture and beat well.

Sift the flour, baking powder, cinnamon, cloves and salt into a bowl, and add a spoon at a time to the egg mixture.

SCRUMPTIOUS CARROT CAKE

4

Stir in the carrot and mix well.

5

Empty the cake mix into the prepared tin and bake in the pre-heated oven for 60-70 minutes or until a skewer comes out clean.

6

Leave the cake in the tin to cool.

7

For the frosting, beat the cheese in a bowl until smooth, add the butter and stir in the sugar.

8

When the cake is cold, spread the frosting on top of the cake and decorate with grated carrot if necessary.

Then slice and enjoy!

LEMON DRIZZLE CAKE

Ingredients...

Makes a 10 x 8 inch (25 x 20 cm) Cake

175g (6oz) butter, softened
175g (6oz) caster sugar
200g (7½ oz) self raising flour
3 eggs
3 tbsp milk

1½ tsp baking powder
finely grated rind of 2 lemons

Topping:
175g (6oz) granulated sugar
juice of 2 lemons

Preparation...

Pre-heat the oven to 160°C (320°F), Gas Mark 3.

Equipment needed...

8 ITEMS

25 x 20 cm (10 x 8 inch) Brownie Tin
Baking Parchment
Medium Mixing Bowl
Electric Whisk
Spatula
Baking Tray
Glass Jug/Mixing Bowl
Dessert Spoon

Method...

1 Line a 25 x 20 cm (10 x 8 inch) brownie tin with parchment paper.

2 Put all the ingredients to make the cake into a medium sized bowl and beat until combined.

3 Turn the mixture into the prepared tin making sure that the mix is pressed into the corners.

LEMON DRIZZLE CAKE

Bake in the pre-heated oven for 25-30 minutes until golden and a skewer comes out clean when inserted.

Leave the cake to cool in the tin for about 10 minutes.

For the topping, mix the granulated sugar and lemon juice in a bowl.

Spoon the mixture over the cake whilst it is still warm, and leave to go cold.

Now enjoy a tangy and moreish slice!

CHOCOLATE CHIP COOKIES

Ingredients...

Makes 24 cookies

190g (6½ oz) self raising flour
100g (3½ oz) light soft brown sugar
140g (oz) chocolate chips
125g (4oz) butter
1 egg

Preparation...

Pre-heat the oven to 180°C (350°F), Gas Mark 4 and line a large baking tray with parchment paper.

Equipment needed...

8 ITEMS

Medium Mixing Bowl
Baking Tray
Parchment Paper
Spatula

Method...

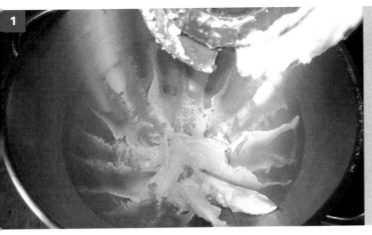

1

Place the butter into a mixing bowl and beat until smooth.

2

Add the egg, flour, sugar and chocolate chips.

CHOCOLATE CHIP COOKIES

Beat all the ingredients together until well mixed.

Make walnut sized balls of the mixture and place on the baking tray, 4cm apart.

Pop them into the pre-heated oven for 9-12 minutes
or until golden brown. Leave to cool on a wire rack.

Perfect with a cuppa!

Annie's CHOCOLATE CARAMEL SLICES

Ingredients...

Shortbread:
150g (5oz) plain flour
50g (2oz) caster sugar
100g (3½ oz) butter

Caramel:
50g (2oz) soft dark
brown sugar

100g (3½ oz) light soft
brown sugar
150g (5oz) butter
1 x 397g (14oz) can condensed milk

Topping:
150g (5oz) chocolate

Preparation...

Pre-heat the oven to 180°C (350°F), Gas Mark 4.

Equipment needed...

7 ITEMS

18cm x 25cm (7 x 10 inch)
Brownie Tin
Parchment Paper
Food Processor
Large Saucepan
Wooden Spoon
Medium Saucepan
Medium Mixing Bowl

Method...

1

Line an 18cm x 25cm (7 x 10 inches) brownie tin with parchment paper.

2

Put the flour and caster sugar into a food processor and add the butter.

3

Pulse the mixture until it binds together.

ANNIE'S CHOCOLATE CARAMEL SLICES

4 Knead to form a soft dough, and roll out onto a lightly floured surface to the size of the tin.

5 Press the shortbread into the tin and bake in a preheated oven 180°C (350°F/Gas Mark 4) for 12-15 minutes, until golden brown.

6 For the caramel, put both the sugars into a non-stick saucepan, add the butter and heat gently, stirring, until melted.

Add the condensed milk and bring to the boil, stirring continuously, until thickened. Pour over the shortbread base, and leave to cool. Place in the refrigerator to chill.

Finally, break the chocolate into a small mixing bowl and place over a pan of boiling water. Stir until melted.

Spread the melted chocolate over the caramel and leave to set.

Cut into slices, then indulge yourself!

BRITISH SCONES

Ingredients...

Makes 6-8 Scones (depending on cutter)

225g (8oz) self raising flour
55g (2oz) butter (cold but
not frozen)
1 level tsp baking powder

150 ml (5 fl oz) milk
A little milk to glaze

Preparation...

Pre-heat the oven to 200°C (400°F), Gas Mark 6, and line a
baking sheet with parchment paper.

Equipment needed...

7 ITEMS

Medium Mixing Bowl
Rolling Pin
5.5 cm round pastry cutter
Pastry Brush
Baking Tray
Parchment Paper
Spatula

Method...

Sieve the flour into a large mixing bowl and add the butter, baking powder and salt.

Rub the butter into the flour with your fingertips until the mixture resembles fine breadcrumbs, working as quickly as possible to prevent the dough becoming warm.

BRITISH SCONES

3

Make a well in the centre and using a cold dinner knife, stir in enough milk to make a soft dough.

4

Turn the mixture onto a floured work surface and very lightly knead until just smooth.

5

Gently roll out dough to 2cm thick. Cut rounds with a 5.5 cm cutter.

6

Place the scone rounds onto the lined baking tray, brush with the beaten egg mixture, and bake near the top of the hot oven for 12-15 minutes or until golden brown and well risen. Cool on a wire rack.

Serve with butter, or lashings of jam and cream!

CHRISTMAS BISCUIT TRUFFLES

Ingredients...

Makes 12 truffles

125g (4¹/₂ oz) digestive biscuits
60g (2¹/₂ oz) butter
2 tbsp golden syrup
1 tbsp milk
30g (1oz) caster sugar
30g (1oz) light soft brown sugar
2 tbsp cocoa powder
1 tbsp drinking chocolate

50g (2oz) raisins
50g (2oz) cranberries
grated rind of ¹/₄ orange
60g (2¹/₂ oz) white
chocolate chunks
40g (1¹/₂ oz) red &
green sprinkles

Equipment needed...

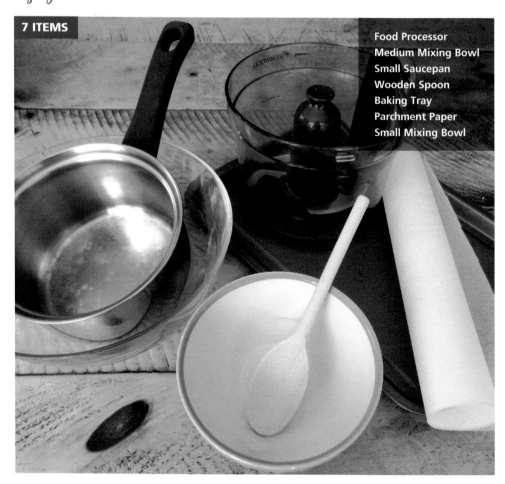

7 ITEMS

Food Processor
Medium Mixing Bowl
Small Saucepan
Wooden Spoon
Baking Tray
Parchment Paper
Small Mixing Bowl

Method...

1 Put the digestive biscuits into a food processor until they resemble fine breadcrumbs, and place in a medium sized mixing bowl.

2 Add the sugars, cocoa powder, drinking chocolate, raisins, cranberries and orange rind to the biscuit crumb and mix thoroughly.

3 Put the butter, golden syrup and milk into a small saucepan and heat gently until melted.

CHRISTMAS BISCUIT TRUFFLES

4

Pour the buttery liquid into the crumb mix and stir until well combined, then place the mixing bowl into the refrigerator for 20 minutes.

5

After it has cooled, make walnut sized balls of the mixture and place them onto a lined baking tray. Place the tray back into the refrigerator.

6

Take the white chocolate chunks and put them into a small mixing bowl. Place the bowl over a saucepan of boiling water and stir until melted.

7

Pour a little of the melted chocolate over the top of each ball, and decorate with the sprinkles.

Then enjoy these little festive delights

DOUBLE CHOCOLATE SURPRISE BISCUITS

Ingredients...

Makes 30-40 biscuits

200g (7oz) butter, softened
165g (5½ oz) caster sugar
150g (5oz) dark brown sugar
½ tsp salt
2 eggs

300g (10½ oz) self raising
flour, sifted
50g (2oz) cocoa powder, sifted
125g (4½ oz) dried Cranberries
95g (3 oz) white chocolate chunks
75g (2½ oz) dark
chocolate chips

Preparation...

Pre-heat the oven to 180°C (350°F), Gas Mark 4, and line
a baking tray with parchment paper.

TIP: As this makes quite a few biscuits, pop the bowl containing the remaining mixture into the fridge, whilst you are waiting for the first batch to cook.

Equipment needed...

7 ITEMS

Medium Mixing Bowl
Electric Whisk
Silicone Scraper
Wooden Spoon
Baking Tray
Parchment Paper
Cooling Rack

Method...

1

Put the butter and sugars into a medium sized mixing bowl.

2

Beat the mixture with an electric mixer until smooth.

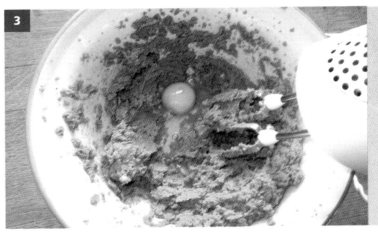

3

Add the eggs one at a time until well combined.

DOUBLE CHOCOLATE SURPRISE BISCUITS

4

Fold in the sifted flour and cocoa powder.

5

Stir the cranberries and chocolates into the biscuit mixture.

6

Place scoops of the mixture, no bigger than the size of a walnut, onto a baking tray, about 3cm apart.

7

Bake the biscuits in the pre-heated oven for about 10-15 minutes or until firm. Leave the biscuits on the baking tray for about 5 minutes before putting them on a wire rack to cool.

Lots to enjoy (and share!)

BAKEWELL TART

Ingredients...

Makes a 9 inch (23cm) tart

Pastry:
115g (6oz) plain flour
pinch of salt
75g (2½ oz) butter
2-3 tbsp cold water

Filling:
100g (4oz) butter, softened
100g (4oz) caster sugar
115g (6oz) self raising flour
1 tsp baking powder
2 eggs
2 tbsp milk
½ tsp almond essence
4 tbsp raspberry jam
2 tbsp flaked almonds

Preparation...

Pre-heat the oven to 170°C (325°F), Gas Mark 3, and lightly grease a 23cm (9 inch) tart tin.

Equipment needed...

9 ITEMS

Food Processor
Medium Mixing Bowl x 2
Measuring Jug
Dessert Knife
23cm (9 inch) Fluted Tart Tin
Rolling Pin
Silicone Spatula
Baking Tray

Method...

1

Place the flour, butter and salt into a food processor until it resembles fine breadcrumbs.

2

Empty into a small mixing bowl and add the water a little at a time using a cold dinner knife, and stir until the dough binds together.

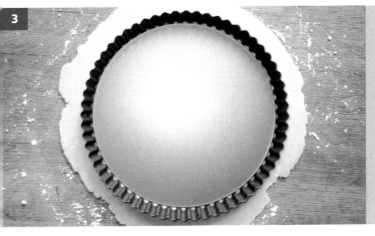

3

Knead slightly, and roll the pastry out on a lightly floured work surface to the size of the greased tart tin.

BAKEWELL TART

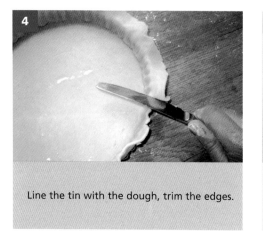

Line the tin with the dough, trim the edges.

Spread the jam over the pastry base and set aside.

To make the filling put the butter, sugar, flour, baking powder, eggs, milk and almond essence into a bowl and mix together until well blended.

Spread the mixture on top of the jam.

Sprinkle with the flaked almonds and bake in the pre-heated oven for about 20-25 minutes or until the top is firm to touch.

Leave to cool in the tin before serving.

Then slice and enjoy!

BANOFFI PIE

Ingredients...

Makes a 9 inch (23cm) pie

1 x 397g (14oz) tin of condensed milk

Pastry:
175g (6oz) plain flour
pinch of salt
75g (2½ oz) butter
2-3 tbsp cold water

Topping:
200ml (6½ fl oz) double cream
2 bananas, sliced
juice of ½ lemon
chocolate, grated to decorate

Preparation...

Pre-heat the oven to 200°C (400°F), Gas Mark 6, and lightly grease a 23cm (9 inch) tart tin.

10 ITEMS

Food Processor
Medium Mixing Bowl x 2
Measuring Jug
23 cm (9 inch) Fluted Tart Tin
Baking Beans
Parchment Paper
Baking Tray
Large Saucepan

Method...

1

Put the tin of condensed milk into a saucepan of water and boil for 1-2 hours. (Remember to top the water up as necessary). Leave to cool.

2

Place the flour, butter and salt into a food processor until it resembles fine breadcrumbs.

3

Empty into a small mixing bowl and add the water a little at a time using a cold dinner knife, and stir until the pastry binds together.

BANOFFI PIE

4

Roll the pastry out on a lightly floured work surface to the size of the tart tin. Use to line the greased tin, and trim the edges. Prick the base and sides of the pastry with a fork.

5

Cover the pastry case with a sheet of parchment paper and fill with baking beans (or uncooked rice).

6

Place on a baking tray and bake in the pre-heated oven for 5-10 minutes. Remove the beans (or rice) and return the pastry case to the oven for a further 4 minutes. Leave to cool.

Spread the caramelised condensed milk over the pasty case.

Place the sliced bananas into a bowl with the lemon juice and gently mix, and place on top of the caramel.

Whisk the cream and pile on top of the bananas, decorate with grated chocolate.

Simply irresistible!

CHOCOLATE PROFITEROLES

Ingredients...

Makes about 24

50g (2oz) butter
150ml (¼ pint) water
65g (2½ oz) plain flour, sifted
2 eggs, beaten
170ml (6 fl oz) double cream, whipped

Icing:
125g (4oz) plain chocolate
15g (½ oz) butter

Preparation...

Pre-heat the oven to 200°C (400°F), Gas Mark 6, and line a large baking sheet with parchment paper.

Equipment needed...

7 ITEMS

Medium Saucepan
Wooden Spoon
Baking Parchment
Baking Tray
Medium (heatproof) Mixing
Bowl
Cooling Rack

Method...

1

In a medium sized saucepan, melt the butter over a low heat and add the water. Bring the liquid to the boil and then take off the heat.

2

Empty the flour into the saucepan and beat well until the mixture leaves the sides of the pan clean. Cool slightly.

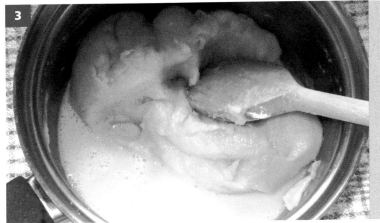

3

Add the eggs a little at a time beating well between each addition.

CHOCOLATE PROFITEROLES

4 Put teaspoons of the mixture onto the baking tray, and bake in the pre-heated oven for 15-20 minutes until crisp and golden brown.

5 Pierce the sides of the profiteroles with a knife to form a small hole (this is to allow the steam to escape), and pop them back into the oven for a further 4 minutes.

6 Take them out of the oven and leave to cool on a wire rack.

7

Fill a piping bag (fitted with a plain nozzle) with the cream and pipe a little into each profiterole.

8

Melt the chocolate and butter in a bowl over a saucepan of boiling water.

9

Dip each profiterole into the chocolate, and leave to set on a wire rack before serving.

*Chocolate
& cream...
just divine!*

CHOCOLATE NOUGAT MOUSSE

Ingredients...

450g (1lb) plain chocolate with Nougat
450g (1lb) double cream
2 eggs
50g (2oz) caster sugar

TIP: Before serving grate some white chocolate over the top of the mousse.

Equipment needed...

5 ITEMS

Medium (heatproof) Mixing
Medium Saucepan
Medium Mixing Bowl
Wooden Spoon
Silicone Spatula

Method...

CHOCOLATE NOUGAT MOUSSE

1 Place the chocolate into a medium heat proof bowl and place over a pan of boiling water. Stir until melted.

2 In another bowl whisk the eggs and the sugar until thick and creamy.

CHOCOLATE NOUGAT MOUSSE

3

In a third mixing bowl, whisk up the cream until sloppy.

4

Add the cream to the egg mixture and stir gently.

5

Fold the melted chocolate into the creamy mixture.

6

Pour into a serving bowl and place in the refrigerator for about 1 hour.

Gloriously light and airy!

LEMON CREAM CHEESECAKE

Ingredients...

Makes a 9 inch (23cm) cake

300g (10½ oz) digestive biscuits
or ginger biscuits, crushed
140g (5oz) butter

Filling:
1 packet of Lemon Jelly
3 tsp water
500g (1lb 2oz) cream cheese
280g (9½ oz) jar lemon curd
125ml (4 fl oz) sour cream

Preparation...

Grease a 23cm (9 inches) loose bottom cake tin.

Equipment needed...

6 ITEMS

Small Saucepan
Wooden Spoon
Medium Mixing Bowls x 2
23 cm (9 inch) Loose Bottom Cake Tin
Dessert Fork

Method...

1

Melt the butter in a small saucepan over a low heat, and leave to cool slightly.

2

Put the crushed biscuits into a large bowl and add the melted butter, and mix well.

3

Empty the biscuit mixture into the greased cake tin and press down and roughen surface with a fork. Place in the fridge for about 15 minutes.

LEMON CREAM CHEESECAKE

Cut the lemon jelly into small pieces and place in a saucepan with the water and melt over a low heat.

In a separate mixing bowl beat the cream cheese with an electric mixer until smooth. Slowly add the jelly liquid, lemon curd and sour cream, and beat until smooth.

5 Remove the flan tin from the fridge, and pour the filling over the biscuit. Refrigerate until firm.

6 Before serving decorate with slices of lemons.

Refreshingly zesty!

Design & Artwork: ALEX YOUNG

Published by: DEMAND MEDIA LIMITED

Publisher: JASON FENWICK

Written by: ANNIE LOW